my h
and yours

For more information, address:
poetry@carmenleanne.ca

FIRST EDITION
ISBN: 978-1-7776197-0-1

Blog:
carmenleanne.ca

my heart and yours

carmen leanne

Hi there, and welcome to my heart and soul.

Throughout the years I have put my heart through far more than necessary; although I must admit, I am thankful for all the sleepless nights because that is where I have found my growth. I have never been one for sharing my story, yet ink splattered pages seem to be the exception. Poetry is supposed to make you feel. The words on the page are meant to take your heart and soul through a roller coaster of emotions, bringing you heartache, love, loss, imagination, and so much more. I believe that no dictionary definition can define true poetry for poetry cannot be placed in a box, it cannot be measured nor defined. Poetry is an arrangement of words that have been tossed and turned with emotion, leaving behind a story in its midst. Poetry can be anything really, and I believe that is why many find beauty within it. Each arrangement of words holds the power to ignite a fire within one's soul, create a waterfall flowing down one's cheeks, or plant seeds for flowers to blossom within. Poetry is not limited to words on a page, it is a story, an experience, it is a glimpse into one's being, their past or present. Behind each poem is not only the author, but each reader who dives in and finds themselves in-between the lines. I hope you enjoy these ink splattered pages and are able to find bits and pieces of yourself along the way. This is my heart and soul upon these pages.

I am now, your open book.

Heartbreak comes in many forms, delivered by many... friends, lovers, family members, and ultimately, ourselves. Love creates an art so breathtaking that when it is stripped from our fingertips we feel as though we are left with a blank canvas, an empty soul. Allowing numbness to replace the beat of our hearts that once created rhythmic waves of motion throughout our veins. This is where I have felt myself floating, and lately, I have allowed myself to wallow in the comfort of everything that is not comforting, creating routines and patterns to escape the void that aches from within. I'd find my fingers sprawled upon the keyboard or my hand gripping the pen, yet the words that usually flow so effortlessly seemed to be lost within. This became my scapegoat. I'd close my laptop or toss the pen aside, breathing out in relief that today was not the day. I was just *too occupied* with more *important* matters that I couldn't take the time to find the right words, or that I just needed *a little more time.* The most assuring lie dipped in honey that I ever told myself was, *you cannot find the words to write because there are no words... you simply don't care. It doesn't matter. It's not worth your time.* And even though I could not find the right words to express my emotions, those words seemed to be enough to soothe the cacophony of my mind. I told myself that I was okay because what was bothering me wasn't consistently on my mind, yet I refused to admit that perhaps the reason it wasn't on my mind was suppression in its purest form-denial. To experience heartbreak is excruciating, yet facing and accepting it can be even harder.

~

Allowing yourself to come to terms with the sudden new reality is not always the easiest truth to swallow, and for the longest time I kept myself farthest from anything that allowed me to feel in an effort to not feel anything at all. Writing has always been a blessing for me because it allows myself to transform as I turn the pages, beginning my chapters with one emotion and finishing with another; however, in order to transform one must first come to terms with the truth, a journey I was not yet ready to partake on. For this very reason I strayed from my passion of words, losing sight of everything that would keep me afloat in an effort to stay blind to the one thing that was trying to drag me under. At this time, I was able to escape the heartbreak from others although it was at the expense of receiving one from myself. I do not know which one is worse. Tonight, I find my fingers dancing upon the keyboard and although the rhythm does not flow as effortlessly as it should, I refuse to let that stop me. I refuse to fall victim to the same emotions, to the same people who once brought such happiness yet left me swallowed in such pain. Time and time again I may lose sight of reality and the joys that follow, yet I will never let that be the closing chapter. My heart heals between the lines of words that will never make it off the tip of my tongue, and that process is far more impactful than heartbreak will ever be.

I hope these pages find you in a state of love and warmth and if not, then I wish for them to leave you in that. I am here to tell you that the path you have wandered alone for so long has come to an end, for I am here to take your hand in mine and we will walk the rest of this beaten path together. We will stray from the given and mold footsteps into the unknown. We will connect the dots and create constellations where once lay a blackened sky, and we will find the beauty that comes within the rolling waves of healing. There is no road map to where we are headed and no destination in mind; although together we will discover the magic in mystery and learn that not all who wander, are lost.

I am now listening to the little voice
Inside my head
I am sorry I pushed you aside
I am sorry I left you alone for so long
But I hear you now
I am listening
I am writing the book

Here is my story and somewhere along the lines, maybe you'll find yours as well.

I may not believe
In love at first sight
But you made it impossible
Not to believe
In love at first something

When your eyes look into mine
It is as though I am waking up
For the very first time

Your name is unknown to my ears
Yet your touch is one remembered
From someplace long ago
And while this body remains foreign
Your eyes
Are not one I'd forget

Your hand clasped in mine
As my eyes are held by yours
Feeling as though they have found
What they have long searched for

Introduced to a stranger
Yet a stranger
You are anything but

- The day we met

You found me in free fall
Unable to grab hold of your hand
You ran to the bottom
Catching me in your arms

- My safety net

What's my biggest fear you ask?

I lean back against the rooftop and gaze into the night sky. Thinking for a moment of spiders, snakes, and scorpions. Then I cast my eyes to the ground below me, dangling my feet over the edge of the roof.

Heights I hear myself say, and you look at me with surprise.

You see, it's complicated. Heights are nothing, beautiful if anything, but the fall... The fall is what scares me.

That moment where time stops as you're spiraling down, losing all of your senses and feeling a loss of direction.

I'm afraid of falling.

Of heavy breathing and pulses racing, of losing your throat in the pit of your stomach and not having control over your very own body.

Heights don't bother me, but falling on the other hand... I'm afraid of falling.

~

The feeling you get when your breath is trapped
inside and your mind becomes a blur.

When nothing else seems to matter because
nothing else exists.

And at this time, I'm afraid of falling.

I look up at you with those striking
green eyes that are watching me ever
so closely and that smile that lights
up your face.

I take in the sound of your voice, sending
an electric current through my body yet at
the same time, calming my every nerve.

I hear your laugh and in a matter of
seconds I'm falling

Falling for you ever so fast, and I don't
think these butterflies in my stomach
can keep me afloat.

What's my biggest fear you ask?
Falling
And I'm falling fast.

My love for you filled every crevasse of
my body with such intensity that I eagerly
searched for words that held the weight
to describe all that you made me feel.

Yet when I went to write my pen sat
silenced upon the paper and it was
then I realized

You are not the letters that make up a
word, you are the spaces in-between
that form a story of their own.

You are the silence that fills the night
when one cannot sleep and the stars
that light up the night sky.

You are the wind that slips through
my walls, playing a tune that twists
around my heart while simultaneously
sending chills throughout my body.

My pen sat silenced upon the paper
for you are not the letters that make
up a word.

You are the spaces in-between that
form a story of their own.

You saw me for who I was
Beneath my surface of insecurities
And for that
I never loved me more
Than when seeing myself
Through your eyes

You Are My Sun

Some say the earth revolves around the sun and that this lifetime is just a door to the next. That our bodies are made up of the same elements forged by stars in the night sky. That you and I, we are one. For when I met you we fell in sync, souls connecting far deeper than this physical realm.

I was told that it's one thing to know someone but another to understand them and you, I understood you as did you to I. For you were my black hole, opening up and swallowing me inside for better or worse we'd be together. Side by side, exploring the universe one galaxy at a time.

Gravity was on our side as luck was not. The hourglass ticking slowly away was running out of time and my love that once held you high did not work for someone who was afraid of falling and falling like a shooting star you did. Falling hard and falling fast for my heart that beat solely for you. Against all odds we fought. Fought against time, the time that was threatening to run out. We fought against doubt, the doubt that rattled our bones and infected our brains, and lastly, we fought against gravity.

~

The same gravity that once pulled us together was now trying to tear us apart.

Our love was an ocean. An ocean so large we could not keep float but we tried, God we tried.

Although it turned out that the right people were not enough for the wrong time, and as I continue on this journey without you by my side I feel empty, because with you I was whole.

But as I lay here looking up at the stars above, I'm reminded that my body is made up of the same elements forged by the stars overhead and it is then that I realize, I am one with the Earth.

I am in the soil that dampens your feet and in the trees that reach for the stars. I am part of the mountains that sculpt your surroundings and in the air that fills your lungs.

I am one with the earth; and therefore, you are my sun.

I was forever searching for myself in someone else. I thought I needed the same passions, personality, hopes and dreams, the same mindset. I thought I needed another me.

When I met you, I convinced myself you couldn't be the one for you and I were not cut from the same stone. As days turned into months and months turned into years, I came to realize that I did not need another me for I was more than complete all on my own. What I needed was everything that I was not.

You and I may not have been cut from the same stone, yet we filled the areas where the other lay cracked. I allowed us to soar and you kept our feet on the ground. Our imaginations we celebrated while you read me chapters I had not yet discovered and I showed you colours your eyes had yet to witness.

This entire time I spent searching for another me, when all I ever needed was you.

- My missing puzzle piece

I went my entire life searching for what I
wanted

But as it turns out, I never knew what I
needed

- Until I met you

I love you I love you I love you.

I want to scream it from the depths of my lungs. I want it to echo through forests and rattle the leaves off of branches.

I love you I love you I love you and the earthquake that follows trembles beneath my toes.

My mind tells me why I shouldn't, my heart begs for me to stop. But the blood rushing through my veins pumps along to the beating of your heart and my soul cannot find another like yours.

I've searched for you in the faces of others and in their touch that they leave, but no matter how far I travel I am always brought back to you. This back-and-forth scrimmage we play is unbearable, but it is nothing compared to your absence.

I want to start over. I want to shake your hand, say your name, and hear mine through your lips. I want to meet you again for the very first time, even though our souls have known the other forever. An old friend, lost throughout time.

I love you I love you I love you I scream from the depths of my lungs, but silence in the echo is all that I hear.

The farther we pull away it seems the
faster we snap back together.
Maybe one day we will finally break

- Forever my elastic band

Right people, Wrong time

I always thought this was an odd saying. I never understood how exterior factors could hold more power than the love and drive that's held within. How time and place could hold more importance than the ones you love. Of course, situations and events can make reality harder for those two people to fall together, but how is it possible that it has the power to prevent it completely. It's not. It shouldn't be. After years of you telling me

It's just the wrong time

I began to ask myself

Then is it really the right person?

Following your heart
Is not an easy thing
Is this a forever
Or is it just a fling
Forever in question
That is you and I
Four years later
I don't want to say goodbye
But this situation
Is not ideal at best
At the heart of it all
We're being put to the test
Pull after pull
And tug after tug
Hearts almost broken
But still you're my drug
Going through rehab
An addict I stay
I still want you
At the end of the day
A friend for forever
A craving for more
I've tried to end it
But can't close the door
Yet after 8 months
My heart needs a break
I think this is best
Yet here I still ache
Aching for you
And all that you are
First kiss years ago
Standing under the stars

~

Wishing to go back
But both we have grown
Together in question
Or apart on our own
They say give it time
But our time is at a loss
Leaving us hoping again
That our paths will once cross
Right person wrong time
Is what you tell me
But is it really the person
If timing's not meant to be?
Happily forever
Is that too much to crave
Up and down with the sea
Crashing like a wave
Yet it's those moments with you
Where the ocean stays still
Happily forever
Together with you I will
But the question is how
And where we go from here
Please help me god
I'll open my ear
Confusion surrounds me
Feeling lost in a maze
But at the end of the day
Being found in your gaze
I know it's been tough
That's not hard to see
But my heart has a lock
And you've got the key

~

You broke down my walls
And helped me stand tall
Reminded me why
Why we went through it all
The ups and the downs
The parting of ways
I want this forever
And not just a phase
I love you I say
Through a whisper at best
But I mean it with all
That lays in my chest
I'm scared of you leaving
But it's not really that
I'm scared there won't be the time
I'm scared of us falling flat
And I know that we won't
But a version of us will
If the pace doesn't quicken
The hourglass will spill
So I guess time will tell
And I'll wait patiently for you
Just don't take too long
For that I can't do

Happy memories flood my thoughts
As I find myself smiling back at us
The years of laughter and love
Now tainted by the memory
Of the 15 months I was yours
While you were someone else's
And I begin to wonder
If any of our memories
Are worth remembering

- Was everything a lie?

I hold onto this belief that you
Are not the monster you portrayed
That if I wait for you
Hold on a little longer
This mask will fall from your face
And I will have you back by my side

In denial that it was you
Who touched my skin
The same day
The same sheets
Where you touched hers
In denial that it was your same mouth
That spoke in words of such love
That simultaneously
Lied with such ease

And in denial that they were your eyes
That watched me trust you without waver
Knowing
I should do anything but

- In denial

Standing in front of the mirror
I stay
Thinking if I look long enough
I will remember
Who I am
My reflection remains foreign
As I look to the past for answers
Searching
For where you left me

Thinking if you come back
Maybe
I will come with you

- If only she knew. You cannot find yourself in the same place you lost yourself

Do not stay for those
Who can only love you in halves
Because you are
Strong
Worthy
Independent
Forever whole
All on your own
And they will leave you believing
That you are not

The light left her eyes as she stared into the night. The darkness took over and swallowed her whole, echoing throughout her empty carcass. Her heart beat quietly and was the only sound to be heard, yet it failed to reach her ears.

The stars

She begged

Please, show me the stars

As she stared into the darkness within.

The world seems to have us programmed
to be attracted to those we cannot have.

The way the moon rises when the sun sets
or how the ocean tide kisses the morning
shore, only to be swept back out to sea.

A rainbow follows the rain while a sunset
will never bask in the light of the stars.

A shadow disappears in the shade and you
my love

You were never meant to stay.

Like a fish on your hook
You dragged me along
Too afraid to let go
But also too afraid to stay
I fought so hard to leave
Except sometimes
I think I fought harder to stay

It's not that you don't love me anymore
It's that you still do
That hurts the most
The fact that you love me
But you love her more
It's the fact that I used to be everything
Until everything wasn't enough.

- Was I ever enough?

Hurting you was never a fear of mine
Because I knew your heart
Was always safe with me
Never to be put
In harm's way

So when you said
Your biggest fear
Was hurting me
That it was the last thing
You ever wanted to do

I should have known
That although it was last
It was still on your list
A box that had already been checked

That your biggest fear
Was not hurting me
But the day
I would find out

- If you didn't want to hurt me, then you wouldn't have.

I watched the matches
Fall from your fingertips
Room by room
My house lit on fire

My heart screamed
Begging me
To put out the flames

But you taught me
That fire
Meant passion

So when my heart
Screamed out in fear
I let her cry

Mistaking it
For love

You left me alone, again.

You told me I had people who cared about me.

That I'd be okay.

I don't know if you were trying to convince me

Or yourself.

She was the moon in disguise
Blessing everyone with light
Yet being left alone
In the shadow of her own.

They're gorgeous she beamed, twirling around with his flags and dancing to a beat that echoed only in her ears.

Her friends and family waved from afar, calling out her name to break her of his spell yet their cries could not overpower the music he had whispered in her ear and with despair, they watched on.

Her feet blistered and bare while wrapped
In his flags of red
Dripping
In her very own blood.

- Toxic Relationships

You danced with me
And spun me around
Our feet
Kissing the floor.
I spun and I spun and I spun
But when the room
Slowed from a blur
You were nowhere to be found
And my feet…

My feet
Were bloody
And bruised.

- Waking up from the music

You told me you loved her
That a part of you always has
How with her
It feels so permanent
My hands wouldn't stop shaking
And for a moment
My heart stopped

I almost threw up

I told you I was fine.

- I slept on the bathroom floor that
night.

The hardest part
Is not letting go
But forgetting
You ever had a grip
In the first place

You're losing me

I would have given you anything and
everything because you were everything
I had ever wanted

The earth, the moon, the stars, they meant
nothing compared to you

And you can't just *forget* a person like that.

Trust me, I would if I could but then again, I
don't know if I'd want to

People say it hurts less to love and to have
lost rather than to never love at all

I still don't know if I agree because loving you
created a happiness in me I did not know
existed, but goddamn the heartbreak that
followed was crippling.

I loved you then and I still do now

I think I always will because you were, and you
are my everything.

You are my person, whether it be as a lover or
a best friend, as long as you are in my life that
is all that matters.

~

I would have given you anything and everything
because I loved you more than the sun that set
for the moon every evening or the ocean that
kissed the shore during the morning tides

And I am truly sorry you could never see or
understand that.

But you're losing me

And I'm terrified because I don't ever want to
experience life without you

Because you are my person, my best friend,
my other half.

But you're losing me, and I'm scared because
I don't know if you just don't notice

Or if you just don't care.

He didn't love you
I hear everyone say.
You don't treat someone you love like that

I heard it over and over again that eventually my heart began to believe it.

You never loved me; you couldn't have...
But at the end of the day, I know in my heart that you did. Maybe it was wishful thinking, wishing that us ending could have been as simple as you not loving me. Maybe it was easier to convince myself you never loved me, rather than acknowledge that you did and were still able to hurt me.

Maybe it was easier to believe you never loved me because then, I wouldn't have to wonder how you were able to leave me.

- A part of me wishes you never loved me

I'm sorry I'm sorry I'm sorry I love you

And he repeated it so many times that the words became foreign to my ears.

They were meaningless

Your photo’s still in my wallet, I can't bring myself to take it out. I'm scared that if I do, then you'll be gone.

It’s funny how minds work that way,
thinking that you're still with me

When we both know

You left long ago

- Maybe tomorrow, I'll try again

But I know him

She whispered as she sank into the floor.

You knew him, but you do not know him

The walls whispered back

Not anymore.

You knew I was scared of heights
And with that you told me to look ahead
Rather than at what lay down below
Knowing
There was no net at the bottom
For you had already snipped it away

My back lay bare
While a parachute
Hid behind yours
Blindly
I held your hand
Letting my foot walk off the edge

Crashing to the bottom
I fell
While you watched from above
My body shatter

I should have known better
Falling for you
After all
If you drop anything from high enough
It will almost always
End up broken

- I'm still trying to put myself back together

For years
I called you my safety net
I just never imagined
You'd be the one
I had to keep myself
Safe from

There was once a time my name spilled
through your lips, sounding like the poetry
held within midnight skies.

Time has since changed and now when
I taste my name on my lips, I do not
recognize it as my own

Because for years it has belonged to you.

There was once a time that was my name

But now is the time when spoken

It feels like it is yours.

She looked me in the eyes and asked

Is he the one?

The memories now kept hidden in the past suffocated me as I relived our time together. Although not as frequent, there are still days I can remember your touch and the sound of your voice as if it were yesterday. My chest felt heavy as I could feel your fingers slip through mine.

He was I whispered back

- Not anymore

We were the static on the radio
The silence when alone
Not a sound to be spoken
Yet a chorus on its own

An unspoken story
The rhythm to a song
Fragile as a feather
But also just as strong

Away we then flew
Creating memories of gold
A fairy tale come true
But our story never told

Written between the lines
Yet missing from the page
We were the stars of the show
Kept hidden backstage

The eye of the tornado
The quiet in the storm
A love kept secret
Never to be mourned

For our souls entangled
Yet our paths did stray
We molded the future
Still somehow lost our way

~

Stranded in the abyss
Is where we were found
Where once hearts sang
Now echoed not a sound

We left us a trail
Of footprints in the sand
But a storm took hold
Now rests an unmarked land

Beauty in the untold
Leaves a secret meant for two
Now that secret is just a story
That the world sure never knew

Memories trapped in time
Kept under lock and key
No trace of the memories
Is that what freedom means

And here I now sit
Silent, I'm alone
Not a sound to be spoken
Our chorus gone to stone

All the promises he never kept and the lies that slipped through his lips

I'll always be there for you
You're my best-friend
I'd never let anyone change who we are
I'll never take you for granted again
I just need time
We can figure this out
It's you and I in the end
You can trust me
I'm sorry
I'm sorry
I'm sorry
I love you

- I still like to think you were telling the truth

I thought maybe if I had the lips of random strangers on mine, I could forget about the taste of yours.

- It never worked

No-one's ever loved me back she whispered
At least, not enough to make them stay.

It was then that I saw a pain buried so
deep behind her eyes, pushed so far
down that if you blink, you'd miss it.

Still somehow, she managed to beam with
such light, as if her eyes hid nothing but
sunshine and rainbows

It hurts because you remember
What was
What could have been
And what no longer is

It's crazy how my body knew
Long before I did
The panic attacks and sleepless nights
For months
You may have had my heart fooled
But my body knew
When your hands
Had been elsewhere

I showered four times
Yet I could still feel
Her lips on yours
And her skin
Beneath your touch.

Was one body not enough?

I still remember our plans that finished before they even had the chance to start. Washed away like our footprints in the sand, almost as if they were never there to begin with.

You see, I questioned everything in life but never you. The same way an infant never questions their mother's love, you were always the one thing in life I was sure of.

- The one thing I should have questioned

It's a horrible thing

Losing yourself in the midst of someone else.

- I'm still trying to find myself

I hear the lies
You tell your friends and family
And most of all, her
Your version sounding so different
Than the one I lived
Ruining my image in an effort
To save your own
The villain in your story
And theirs I stay
Painting the picture
You want them to believe

How ironic
When that's the same
You did to me

- I don't blame you. I wouldn't want them to know the real you either

I had been left in darkness for so long that when I saw a light appear in the distance, I ran eagerly towards it with open arms.

Too blinded

To see

It was a train

- I thought you were the light at the end of my tunnel, I had never been more wrong.

She poured her heart and soul onto
paper for the pages understood her
better than any other.

Or maybe she turned to paper because
the words on the page were the one
thing that would never leave.

Maybe it was because she could write
the words, she was too afraid to say.

Maybe by writing she could convince
herself the words were for anyone,
but her.

I blocked your number
Not to keep you away
But because it was easier to go to bed
Wondering if you tried to call

Than go to bed knowing you never did.

I crave love.

To love, and to be loved.

Yet when I look in the mirror I do
not know if after all this, if I truly
believe in love.

I see the love shared by elders that
grows stronger with age.

And I know that I love the moon and
the rain and the stars in the night sky.

I know that my sister loves her fiancé
and my teacher loves his wife.

But when it comes to me
I can't picture anyone loving me.

You said I love you my dear
But I'm sorry it's not so
I just got caught in the moment
Started putting on a show
And now I'm parting my way
I don't want to hear from you
Yea it was fun while it lasted
Now there's nothing I can do

- I put you in a song

And it was in that moment my heart stopped.

The moment the birds fell quiet, the wind
stayed still, and the buzz of the world
disappeared.

Now is normally when I would hear the
beat of my heart pounding against my rib
cage but all that came was the blood

Pumping through my veins.

- June 25th. A piece of me died that day

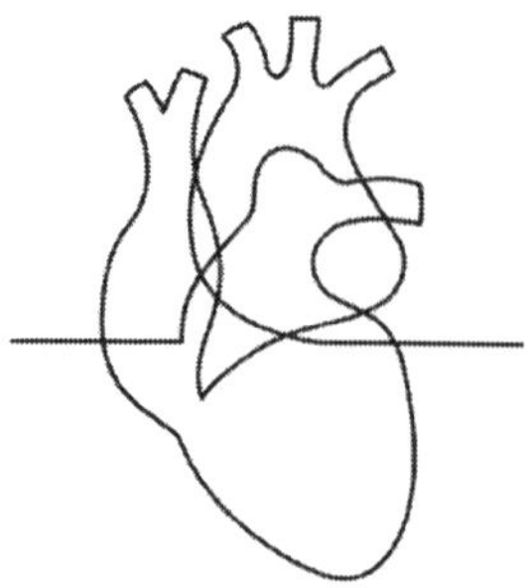

Missing you is something
I've grown used to

There are still days
I believe this is all
A bad dream
That I will wake-up to the rhythm
Of your chest
Rising with every breath
As your arms pull me tighter
And our legs intertwined

- Please let me wakeup

I will never regret loving you
But I will forever regret
Not leaving sooner

You whisper in my ear
While your fingers trace my skin
A roadmap of lies you create
You give me a kiss
And I lick my lips
Finding salt
Never tasted so sweet

You painted a picture so sweet
That when my friends and family
Begged me to open my eyes

I argued they were never closed

Ever so slowly
Is how you took from me
Stripping me down
Then giving me back in pieces
Tricking me into thinking
Those parts of myself
Were gifts from you
So grateful to receive
That I fell blinded
To what was missing
It wasn't until you left
That I found myself standing
In an empty room

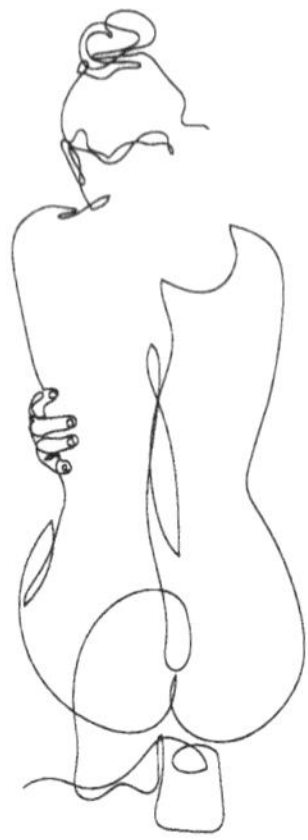

You have not lost anything, you escaped.

Do not mistake the two

We don't talk anymore.
I know it's probably for the best
But I can't help wondering
If you still think of me

If you miss our late-night conversations
If you miss my arms around yours
I tell myself if you wanted to
You would reach out

You probably tell yourself the same thing

How is it that you can leave me so
broken and bruised yet I still find
myself searching for the same arms
that hurt me, to hold me.

- My comfort in the pain, even when that
  pain is you

I knew you weren't healthy for me
At least not right now
You used to bring me such light
Yet my days were now cast in shadows

Everyone always asks
Why I never left sooner
I knew you brought darkness
But there was such beauty
When the light shone through
That I forgot
Stained glass
Still shatters

Once more I took his hand
Allowing him to paint a new reality
One far prettier than this

I put the blindfold on and let him
Lead the way
I had the steps memorized
For he never led me anywhere new

I do not know why I find it so hard
To walk away
When I am standing in nothing but ruins
Maybe I think if I stay long enough
A flower will rise from the ashes
And just like the flower
We could try again

But what I fail to realize
Is even if the flower rises from the ashes
It will still stay surrounded
In nothing
But ruins

- Maybe it is time to plant my flower
  elsewhere

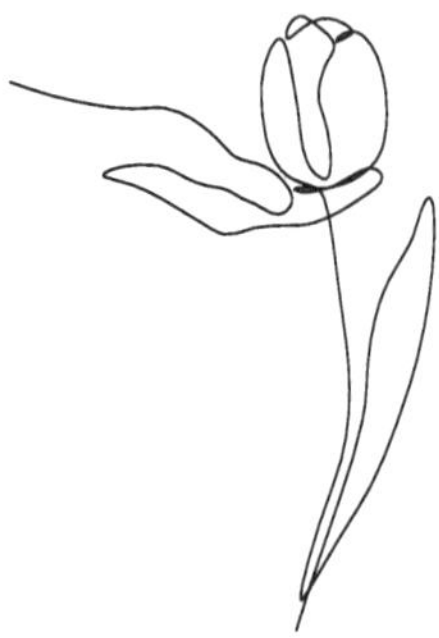

And even after all this time
I still think you are a good person
And I do not know if that is called love
Or manipulation

- Perhaps it is both

I'm too much she whispered.

People come as quickly as they leave.
Salivating at the lips, begging for a taste of
her mystery. A mystery wrapped around
ever so tightly, a never-ending maze.

It's an optical illusion she says

You see, they beg for love, becoming so blinded by their own desires they fail to see the lust before their very own eyes. The reality they conjure is nothing more than a mere mirage meant to feed their hunger and once they've been fed, they'll disappear.
They always do.

I know I am capable of love.
I know that I can love, and that I will
be loved; however, you let me believe
that no one will ever love me enough.

- Why aren't I enough

I told you more times than I can
count that I was leaving.
That I could no longer wait for you.

I came back every time.

- I'm not coming back anymore

I know I'll be okay
I know I'll meet someone new
And the memory of you will slowly fade
I know this pain will disappear
And soon I won't wince
At the sound of your name
I know that this is for the best
And that one day
One day I'll be okay

I put so much energy into loving you
That I forgot to love myself along the way

In front of the mirror she stood
Staring at the woman in front of her
Broken
Time and time again

But here you are
Rebuilding yourself
Once more

I love you

She whispered

Even if no-one else will

I used to keep my porch light on
With the hopes of you
Finding your way home

Yet I no longer stayed awake for you
As I knew I'd be waiting forever

Still the porch light stayed on
Until the sun rose each morning

You never showed up then
Why would it be any different now

- I think tonight I'll turn my porch light off

You dug a hole so deep
You gave up on climbing out
And instead
Hoped if you dug far enough
You'd come out
The other side

- I'm afraid you're only deeper

Somehow you managed to break my heart and blame me in the process. I am sorry if you got hurt by hurting me, but you cannot blame me for your actions. They are yours to own.

I was hurt by you.

You were hurt by the choices you made

Not because of me

- There is a difference, I am not the one to blame.

You can't explain a love like ours.
Words don't do it justice.

Love at first sight
Soul Mates
True love

It wasn't any of the above
We were so much more than that.

Maybe that's why
We didn't work
Maybe we couldn't have
Maybe we were too much
For this world to handle

- We were too much for us to handle

They keep telling me that if you wanted to
you would. That not hearing from you is
an answer in itself.
That if you wanted to, you would.

I say that's not always the case.
Sometimes people want to
But they don't have the courage.
Sometimes the pain is too much to bear.
Sometimes they want to
They just don't know how to.

After all, you haven't heard from me either

I love you.

But there is only so much you can do
for someone who isn't willing to love
you back

A knight in armour you stood
Allowing me the rights
To my own body
How sad it is
That I admired you
For a thing such as that

Standing there proud
You beamed
Seeking a reward
As if I should praise you
For not taking
What was never yours

I begged you to hurry back
Only because I was weak enough
To let you in again
And I knew if you gave me time
I would develop the strength
To finally lock the door

It is not that I don't believe in love; in
fact, it is quite the opposite. I am so
mesmerized and infatuated with love.

I believe that two people can love one
another and that I can love someone
else, but what I struggle to believe is
that someone could ever love me.

I have been shown time and time
again from men who were supposed
to love me that I was either not
enough, or they struggled with
showing love themselves and in
return, I carried the burden.

It is not that I don't believe in love,
but if the men who were supposed to
love me growing up never did

Then why would I expect anyone else to.

I still have you as an emergency contact
Maybe it's foolish
But I just can't imagine them
Calling anyone else

- You're still the one I'd call

I know I'll move on
I know that one day I'll wakeup
And you won't be the first thing
That comes to mind
I know that I'll meet someone else
Someone new
Someone that will love me
As much as I love them
I know that you and I
Weren't meant for forever
But there are still times
I wish we were

It took me a long time to accept that
no love will ever be like ours.

- And that is okay

Her ears start to ring as he repeats the line she knows all too well. Fingers trembling as she watches him leave as easily as he came-gone with the wind. Cheeks facing the sky, she begs the clouds for answers

Why am I never enough?

Raindrops kiss her skin as they sing

But darling, you will be more than enough for the one who matters. Give it time. You are all and more than what you will ever need to be. Breathe.

And so she did, and so she was

All and more, than what she ever needed to be.

I'll never be the same person
I was
Before I met you

But I'll be okay

- I promise

I am sorry, I say to the mirror.

You fell in love and experienced such pain that your heart should not have felt for many more years to come. You spent your teenage years mourning over something that never was but could have been. I am so sorry I let it drag on for so long. That I didn't stand up for you, but I am here now. I won't ever let you wither away while trying to save a love the other does not wish to save.
I am here and I am sorry. I love you.

A message to my 16-year-old self

A part of me wishes we never met
But I know that is not true.
I'll never forget you
And as much as a part of me
Wishes that I could
I know I would never want to.

You told me I needed to stop writing
about you. That you had moved on and
were happily involved with someone else.
That it wasn't nice of me.
I wanted to scream from the depths of
my lungs.

You stole everything from me.

You are not allowed to steal my words
as well.

- You did this to me. You do not get
a say in how I choose to heal

I forgive you
But that does not mean
I've forgotten
How you treated me

Words weaving through my mind
But the pages staying bare
My thoughts a rushing current
No sanity to be spared
Merging in from reality
Then out to the sea
I try to stay afloat
And this you must believe
Some days the rapids rest
And the waters flow with grace
But then I'm crashing into rocks
Can't seem to find my place
The ups and the downs
And the stories they share
I try to move on
Don't fit here nor there
So I stay feeling stuck
With my memories of you
Please help me someone
Tell me what can I do
And I hear from afar
A whisper to say
You must take some time
Leave the wounds at bay
And so I write my own story
Continue staying strong
One foot after another
For who knows how long
But I leave faith in the unknown
As I guess that I must
Hoping it'll get better in time
In that, I do trust

Self-love is the hardest to give
But the most important to receive

She loved fairy tales
And perhaps that is why she fell hard
And she fell fast
Perhaps she was falling for what could be
Instead of what actually was

Blinded by rose coloured glasses she stood
Time after time again
And there she would stay

Heart on her sleeve
And hope in the air
Blinded
By rose coloured glasses

He whispered sweet little nothings
Into her ear
But sweet little nothings
Is all that they were.

They ask if I have moved on and the words get
caught on my tongue

I want to ask what moving on looks like to them

If they are asking if my cheeks are no longer
stained from flowing tears

If they are asking if your profile is no longer
the first thing I check when the sun rises

Or if they are asking if I can be alone without
crumbling to the floor

And if those are the answers they are looking
for then the answer is yes, I have moved on

But if they are asking if after all this time, I have
stopped waiting for your call

If they are asking if I have finally admitted that
it is over, ready to walk away

Or if they are asking if I can look out my window
without hopes of seeing you pull into my
driveway

And if those are the answers they are looking for
then the answer is no, I have not

And I am afraid I never will

- My heart still skips a beat when my phone rings

The betrayal from you
Left an ache in my body
I do not yet know
How to soothe

Some days, flowers will blossom
from your touch and birds will sing
to the sound of your voice.

Other days, oceans will pour from
your eyes and the world will crumble
beneath your feet.

Both are okay.

They say love is a drug and that is the very reason your name no longer dances upon the tip of my tongue.

- I cannot risk another relapse

Maybe one day we will meet again, and things will be different

I wanted to scream and shake him till
his bones rattled against their cage.

The world doesn't work that way!
Don't you know life doesn't get
handed to you on a golden platter?
Don't you know that if you want
something, you have to fight for it?

Maybe that was my answer.

Maybe he never wanted me at all.

Maybe this was just his way of telling me.

When I had to convince
My friends and family
That our relationship was healthy
That is when I should have known
It wasn't

- The *first* red flag

I am told they always come back
When the dust has settled
And they realize what they had

But this is different
Because I did not simply
Pass you by

You held my hand
Looked in my eyes
And still chose
To say goodbye

- You always knew what you had.
  You still chose to walk away

I am not quite sure
What changed
All I know is that life
Is precious
And I had spent far
Too many months
Wrapped around your finger
Walking on eggshells
And celebrating days
I did not cry
Time waits for no one
And you had already stolen
So much of it from me
I refuse to let you steal
Anymore

- Time to dry the tears

I never loved me more than when seeing
myself through your eyes and perhaps that
was my problem all along

Perhaps that is why you leaving brought
such pain

Perhaps that is why I found it so hard
to love myself without you here

- It's time I started loving myself without
  seeking permission from others

I was so afraid to let go
Because I thought no-one
Would ever love me
Like him

How blinded I was
For she took my hands and whispered

Darling.

I pray that no-one ever "loves" you, like that again

- Love should not destroy you

You're never going to get over me, will you

he asked

No

I said while fiddling with his fingers
intertwined with mine

But you don't want me back either, do you...

No, not anymore

I whispered back

- You came to me in a dream

Perhaps it is not an ending, but a beginning.

The beginning of something so much better

Than what was left behind.

Don't get lost in her eyes
For you'll forget to breathe
Within the maze of the forest
You'll never be free
The depths of green
And the stories they share
One look from her
And it's too much to bear
Your lungs start to wheeze
Your heart breaks its cage
The wisdom she holds
Goes far past her age
Her voice rattles your thoughts
Nothing else can be heard
The world around you
It all becomes blurred
For her touch starts the storm
That quickens your breath
Though all the same time
Stops it like death
Don't get lost in my eyes
You hear her plea
But it's too late for that
They're all that you see

- They say that the eyes are the
  windows to the soul

We sat on the swings where memories of
late-night talks reside in the waters

Ingrained within the sand

We make small talk

Ask the other how their day has been, how
the last few years have treated us

Everything we should already know
but no longer do

I don't know how we got here.

How after all this time we find ourselves
on the same swings

Yet tonight we are strangers.

I look out to the water and find myself more
comfortable in silence

Than in conversation.

There was once upon a time that the very sound of your name brought shivers down my spine. A time where the rhythm of your voice allowed for the pumping through my veins and a time where all of me was consumed, by all that was you.

Times have changed. Your touch now falls foreign upon my skin, your voice is but one in the crowd, and my lips, my lips do not remember the taste of your name.

- I am free

I spent years wishing and fighting for you

When all along

I should have been fighting for myself

I do not want you to blame yourself.

I want you to face your demons and face
your actions and grow through that.

I want you to make those difficult choices
you were always too afraid to make and I
want you to stand up for yourself.

I did not deserve what you did to me

But I do not want you to blame yourself.

I want you to grow.

I want you to make sure you never do to
someone else

What you did to me.

I don't blame you

A few years ago

I didn't know if I could live without you

- I'm thriving

You are allowed to mourn for what you
have lost, even if what you lost was merely
an illusion of what you thought you had.

You are allowed to crave the companion of
a friend who turned out to be anything but

You are allowed to miss the relationship
that was not always healthy

And you are allowed to grieve from the pain
or trauma that others do not understand

You are allowed.

When someone truly loves you, you won't have to question it

- The only thing you told me that wasn't a lie

I will always be there *for* you
Whether it be next week
Or ten years from now
A promise I made
Many years ago
Still stands strong
In even the worst of storms
But I can no longer
Be there *with* you
And for that
I am sorry

- I will miss you, always

Darling, you will never be *too much*
For the one who wants you to be
Their everything.

I kept thinking
That all those times you came back

It was because you loved me

What I never considered
Was that maybe you kept coming back

Because you loved how I made you feel

About yourself

Maybe it was never
About me at all

I still wonder how you're doing
But that's not my place anymore

The rays from the sun dance forth upon the moon. She welcomes him with open arms, allowing his touch to travel across her skin, illuminating the trail he leaves. He falls careless. Taking her trust and pressing too deep, leaving craters of emptiness upon her once smooth skin. He leaves as swiftly as he came, blanketing darkness where once was light.

The darkness she soon thanked for without the lack of light she would never have found her own. She pooled the craters with love and allowed herself to bathe within. Acceptance of the past, present, and future washed over as regret washed away. She smiled at the thoughts that once brought tears and she laughed at what once was pain. She stood brave and tall and with that she shone through the night, never to lose her light again.

Tread gently on my soul she begged.

He looked into her eyes and found himself within solar systems, shooting stars, and black holes. An everlasting fire burned down to her core.

He was lost within
Yet he'd never felt more at home.

Do not leave the door unlocked
For those who willingly
Walked out.

They do not get to come and go
As they please.

My body no longer calls your touch home.

As much as I want to hate you, I can't. I understand why you held on for so long and why you refused to let me walk away. I don't hate you, but I am disappointed. I once held so much admiration for you and so much respect. You were the type of person I strived to be. I understand why you treated me the way you did, and I can't hate you for that even if it was far from okay. But I do not look up to you anymore because of it.

- You are not the same person from when I first met you

We will meet again.
If not in this life
Then the next.

- I am sure of it

If you would have asked me to describe life
a couple years, or even just months ago, I
would have compared it to a tsunami.
Dragging you along in its bitter cold waters,
bringing you up just to slam you back down
again. Leaving you in a lost state of mind
filled with confusion and horror.

Ask me the same question today and I will still
tell you life is a tsunami, although I no longer
label it as bitter cold waters of lost directions
but a majestic force working together in
rhythmic motions that echo in ups and downs.
And the waters are no longer bitter cold,
they're refreshing and awakening.

It is not life itself that changes
But our perspectives that do.

I had to learn to love myself as much
as I once loved you

One day you will no longer feel the weight of
the world as a burden for you to hold.
One day you will no longer daydream of a
new reality.
One day you will no longer feel the need to
search for yourself in others.

One day, you will see.

You will see that the weight of the world is
lighter when shared with others, yet you will
know you are equally capable of carrying it
on your own.
You will see that there is no need to
daydream because your current reality is a
dream within itself, and you will see that you
are anything and everything you may ever
need to be.

That you are entirely full
All on your own.

One day, you will see.

You are worth so much more
Than a backup plan
And if they cannot see that
It is their loss
Not yours.

- Do not forget this

You are loved.

By the soil that finds home between the creases of your toes to the rain that parts from the clouds above.
By the sun whose rays dance down upon your neck and by the trees that lend shade when the heat is too much to bear.
You are loved by the crashing of ocean waves and the thunder that ignites the sky, by the birds flying north to the critters burrowing below.
You are loved each day that turns the world round and the nights where everything is left still, yet never more alive.
The early mornings filled with coffee and the late nights where the sun finds a place to rest.

Yes you, my dear, radiant soul

You are loved. You are loved. You are loved.

Understand that you are allowed to love someone and not want them back.

Know that it is okay to miss the memories but not the person.

And remember that no matter how much time has passed, you are allowed to cry for what you have lost.

- Things to remind yourself

Her cheeks were soaked with saltwater
And although she felt she were drowning
She was merely watering her roots
Getting ready to bloom
Once more.

I never realized how toxic our relationship
was until you left.

I loved you more than anything I ever could
and because of that I emptied myself while
giving to you.

I may have walked away a shell of what I
once was

But I have rebuilt myself into the woman
that I am today.

- I am so proud of her

My heart does not know
How to love
In small measures
Time and time again
I beg for her
To slow down
Build a wall
To love less
She laughs in return

But darling

Have you heard laughter from a child
A bird's song come morning
Rain drops pitter patter upon the Earth's floor

Love is everywhere
And I refuse to experience it
Anything but fully

And when it rains
Perhaps it is not about
What is being washed away
But what hides beneath the surface
Being watered
Waiting
To grow

I am a sunflower.

My sun is no longer a person. My sun is no longer society's impossible demands. My sun is no longer what others say is right or what others say is wrong. My sun is my energy and the rays lead me to whichever direction the wind blows. I have risen from the dirt below and I reach with open arms to the sky above. The chorus in my life is sung by birds welcoming the dawn of a new day, a brighter day, even when the clouds float through. My petals are the stories that make up my past, present, and future. Each event blessing this flower with a bigger and brighter surface, a deeper story to tell. I have been wakened by the rivers that flow through my roots, teaching me how to swim even when my feet cannot find the ground. I am blessed with the rainbows that showers bring and the calm that comes after a storm.

I am a sunflower, and I am now looking towards my own sun.

And up like a rose I will rise.

Pushing through the dirt and reaching for
the sky above.

My past experiences no longer restrict me,
rather they hold my roots in place as I stand
strong, face towards the sun.

Finding myself
In the rhythm of the wind.

Her voice carries the sing song of the doves
and her breath glides along like the wind.

She stands as tall as a great oak yet humbled
by her roots.

Her shadow falls behind for the sun is all
she sees, and the clouds part for her to
stay.

You can wait and with effort decipher her
tune or untangle her roots

But the spirit of hers
Will never be tamed.

Just like a tree from its roots, a flower from a seed, I will blossom into all that was set out for me.

I will grow into a web of wonders
And I will be free.

You were not weak for the nights you had
to sleep on the bathroom floor, cradling
the toilet with fears of throwing up.
You were not weak for having to hide in
a bathroom stall, crying between classes.
You were not weak for all those times
you went back to him.
You were not weak for taking 5 years
to finally walk away.
You were not weak, you were strong.
You were strong for having that much
pain in your heart and yet still managed to
get up and concur the day.
You were strong for all the nights you
cried yourself to sleep but still made your
bed in the morning.
You were strong for fighting so hard for
what you believed in.
You were strong for not giving up
when every part of your aching heart
begged you to.

You were not weak, you were strong.

You are a fighter

I am coming to peace with myself.
I am falling in love with all that I was
All that I am
And all that I will be.

If you can't seem to reach me anymore
It is not because I am lost
It is because I am finally found

I no longer find myself in distress of what was, what is, or what may be. I no longer look to the past for hints of the future and I no longer linger within wishes for the unknown. I often found myself living in an alternate reality, one where my past was molded by my own two hands and shaped into my desires, even when those same desires were causing pain hidden between the shadows of hope. Sometimes what we need is to lose everything, for that is when we realize not everything has been lost. The toxicity of wandering through mazes of past lifestyles and habits is one we all know a little too well. Following my footsteps led me only to where I have always been, and not to where I dreamt of going. The path ahead may be full of bristles and thorns although that is only because this is your path to shape, and I have accepted that you cannot mend and transform your future while trying to transform your past. I have let rest what does not beg to wake, and I have reached out to the path ahead with eager hands, ready to be bruised while exploring; the thorns and bristles being the hardships that lead to the clear meadow ahead.

I am ready.

I am better than I was yesterday
But maybe better than I will be tomorrow
And that is okay
Healing comes in waves
And slowly
I am learning to swim

Saltwater tears feed the rivers rushing through my veins, watering the very roots that allow me to stand tall, face towards the sun. Some days like tonight however, my shadow feels too much to bear. I call for the sun yet refuse to open my eyes because sometimes sorrow feels better when wallowed in. Saltwater tears hold the power to strengthen within yet overflowing into pools I let them be, drowning in the very same currents that beg me to dance. It is in these moments I write.

My soul feels empty and my body numb yet my fingers lit with a spark, begging to ignite the fire within. I've spent years asking myself questions I already knew the answers to and even longer pretending those answers ceased to exist. Countless poems fill my journals, computers, memories ... searching for the one that will set me free. I write to comprehend yet often I am left wondering if comprehension is merely a mirage. A mirage we feed ourselves out of despair to fulfill our everlasting desire to be in control.

~

I struggle to find words to write upon this page as my heart rests empty, numb. I suppose sometimes that's alright. To pull words from emotions and string them along a page is a magical thing; however, it is also just as magical to let those emotions be felt. To allow all that there is to wash over you. Allowing the sea salted waters to trickle into rivers upon our skin, decorating this canvas of our own.

I write to heal, to dream, to breathe, to feel. The words may not always come yet slowly the waves stop crashing, the currents begin to slow, and the sun peaks out from behind the clouds. It is now that I begin to dance in the very same currents that once took hold of my breath. It is now that I send the pools of saltwater tears back to my roots, allowing me to stand tall and brave, and it is now that I open my eyes

Saying hello to the sun

The 5 Steps to Happiness

Acceptance

Accepting whatever it is that is making you uneasy or the emotions that are keeping you from where you want to be. Accept the emotions you're going through, do not try to deny them.

Acknowledgment

Acknowledging why you are feeling that specific way and asking yourself what it is trying to tell you. What does it want you to learn.

Movement

Learning to move forward and to let go of whatever emotions you do not want by your side. Whatever is not benefiting you, let it go.

Growth

Growing from what you have experienced and what you have learned. Channeling the positive out of the situation and using the negative as learning experiences for the future.

Continuation

Continuing on that path of growth, putting one foot in front of the other. Do not be afraid to take it day by day.

Your mind is a garden. Plant and water what you want to grow.

Heartbreak is never easy and rebuilding yourself after can be even harder; however, without those troubling times I would not have been able to create this book, and for that I am thankful for everything I have gone through. I would like to say thank you to the individuals who are written between these lines. I have found peace with each of you and my poetry has blossomed because of our stories, and I am forever grateful for that. I would like to thank mom for holding my hand throughout this journey and wiping my tears when I no longer could, you have been my rock through it all. I would like to thank the individuals who have believed in my writing since the beginning, showing me the endless support that has given me the power to continue telling my story; and finally, I thank Sophie Sherry. The one who reminded me of who I am at the root of all the chaos. For when I put down my pen she picked it back up and told me to write. I will forever thank you for that, for reminding me of who I am. These past six years have been one crazy journey and as difficult as they have been, I would not be the individual that I am today without them. Thank you

Thank you.

Made in the USA
Las Vegas, NV
04 April 2021

20791543R00094